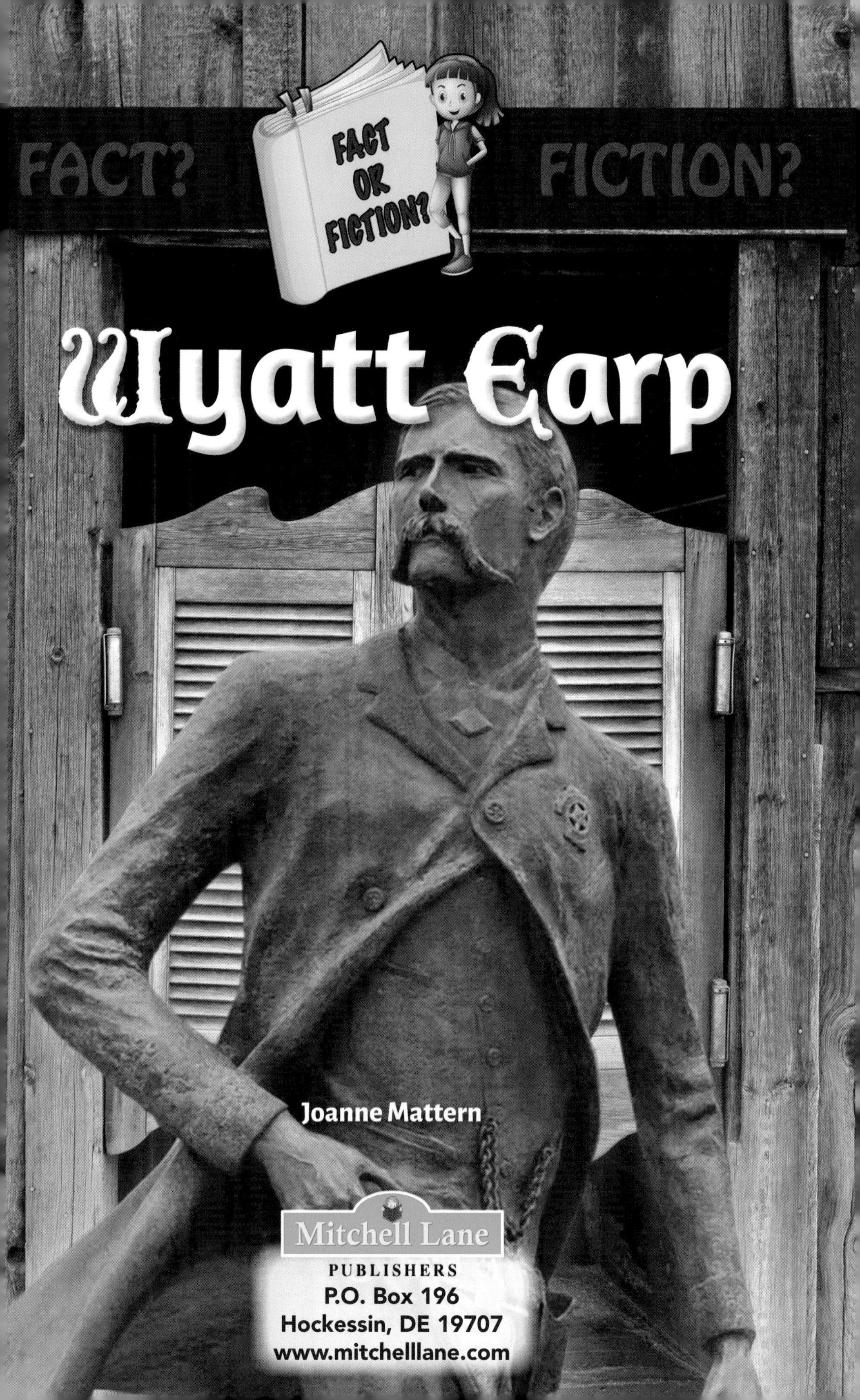

Wyatt Earp

Joanne Mattern

Mitchell Lane
PUBLISHERS
P.O. Box 196
Hockessin, DE 19707
www.mitchelllane.com

Mitchell Lane
PUBLISHERS

Printing   1   2   3   4   5   6   7   8

Audie Murphy   Francis Marion
Buffalo Bill Cody   Robin Hood
The Buffalo Soldiers   The Tuskegee Airmen
Eliot Ness   **Wyatt Earp**

Library of Congress Cataloging-in-Publication Data
Mattern, Joanne, 1963–
   Wyatt Earp / by Joanne Mattern.
      pages cm. — (Fact or fiction?)
   Includes bibliographical references and index.
   ISBN 978-1-61228-958-8 (library bound)
   1. Earp, Wyatt, 1848–1929—Juvenile literature. 2. Peace officers—Southwest, New—Biography—Juvenile literature. 3. United States marshals—Southwest, New—Biography—Juvenile literature. 4. Southwest, New—Biography—Juvenile literature. 5. Tombstone (Ariz.)—History—19th century—Juvenile literature. I. Title.
   F786.E18M38 2015
   978'.02092—dc23
   [B]
                                                                    2015010443

eBook ISBN: 978-1-61228-959-5

                                                                              PBP

CONTENTS

Words in **bold** throughout can be found in the Glossary.

In 1881, a legendary gunfight took place at the O.K. Corral in Tombstone, Arizona. The battle turned lawman Wyatt Earp into an outlaw. It also left three men—Billy Clanton and brothers Frank and Tom McLaury—dead.

O. K. CORRAL
FEED & LIVERY STABLES
HORSES, MULES, BOUGHT, SOLD, & TRADED
HAY & GRAIN. HORSE SHOEING. BLACKSMITH WC
MULE & OX SHOES MADE TO ORDER.
John Montgomery owne
1881

CHAPTER 1

Gunfight!

It was three o'clock in the afternoon on October 26, 1881. Eight armed men were about to confront each other in an empty lot near the O.K. **Corral** in Tombstone, Arizona. Three were brothers. Their names were Wyatt, Virgil, and Morgan Earp. Virgil Earp was the **marshal** of Tombstone. His two brothers were his **deputies**. Wyatt's best friend, Doc Holliday, also walked with the brothers.

Facing them were the Clanton brothers, Ike and Billy, and their friends, Frank and Tom McLaury. The Clantons and the McLaurys were part of a gang that had been making trouble in Tombstone.

Like many Wild West towns, Tombstone was a very rough place. Josie Marcus, who later married Wyatt Earp, said a common saying about Tombstone was that the town "had a man for breakfast every morning, meaning someone was killed every night."[1] The Clantons and the McLaurys were some of the most violent men in Tombstone, and it was up to the Earps to stop them from making more trouble.

That morning, Ike Clanton had stalked the streets of Tombstone carrying pistols and a rifle. He said that there would be a shootout that day.

Now it looked like the shooting was about to start. The town's sheriff, John Behan, was standing near the **outlaws**. He asked them to give up their guns, but the gang ignored him. The Earps and Holliday edged closer and closer. When they stopped, the two groups were only six feet apart. Sheriff Behan and another gang member named Billy Claiborne hid inside a store. They knew trouble was about to start.

No one knows who fired the first shot, but in seconds the street was alive with gunfire. Wyatt shot Frank McLaury, and Morgan shot Billy Clanton. Doc Holliday shot Tom McLaury. Meanwhile, Ike Clanton ran into a store and escaped through the back door.

Even though they were injured, Billy and Frank kept on shooting. Billy shot Virgil in the leg, and Frank hit Doc in the hip. Then Morgan shot Frank. A second later, Billy Clanton shot Morgan. Morgan and Wyatt fired at Billy until he collapsed. Even though he was dying, Billy begged someone to give him more bullets for his gun.

The gunfire only lasted for thirty seconds. When the smoke cleared, Billy Clanton, Frank McLaury, and Tom McLaury lay dead. Doc Holliday and Virgil and Morgan Earp were injured, although not seriously. Only Wyatt Earp was not hurt.

Several days later, Sheriff Behan charged all of the Earps and Doc Holliday with murder. The four men were eventually cleared of the charges. However, the Gunfight at the O.K. Corral changed everything for the Earp brothers. Within six months, Virgil would be seriously injured, Morgan would be dead, and Wyatt would be an outlaw.

Today the O.K. Corral is a tourist attraction. Here, modern-day actors replay the famous gunfight.

The Gunfight at the O.K Corral is one of the best-known gun battles in American history. It became a symbol of the violence and lawlessness that ruled the streets of many Western towns. Many years later, the fight also made Wyatt Earp an American hero. He came to stand for fearlessness, loyalty, and standing up for what was right no matter what the cost.

However, Wyatt Earp was not entirely a hero. During his life, he was on the wrong side of the law several times. Even though he was a lawman, he could also be a cold-blooded killer. Let's meet the real Wyatt Earp and learn what parts of his legend are fact—and what parts are pure fiction.

Wyatt Earp at age 21. By that time, he had already worked on a wagon train, as a stagecoach driver, and a mule handler for the Union Pacific Railroad.

CHAPTER 2

Wyatt Wanders

Wyatt Berry Stapp Earp was born in Monmouth, Illinois, on March 19, 1848. His parents, Nicholas and Virginia Ann, already had three sons: Newton, James, and Virgil.

Wyatt's brothers Morgan and Warren were born a few years later. Wyatt also had three sisters: Virginia, Adelia, and Martha.

When Wyatt was just two years old, the family moved to a farm in Pella, Iowa. They moved several more times during Wyatt's childhood. Wyatt's father believed that good men should stand up for what was right, no matter what the cost. He had served as a lawman when the family lived in Monmouth, and also fought in the Mexican-American War. However, Nicholas was also a heavy drinker and a bully who sometimes left town rather than pay a debt. Historian Andrew Isenberg commented, "I think that being Nicholas Earp's son was not an easy thing."[1]

In 1861, the United States was torn apart by the Civil War. Nicholas Earp joined the Union Army, along with his three oldest sons. Thirteen-year-old Wyatt stayed home to run the farm, but he was bored and

Wyatt Earp and his large family grew up in this house in Pella, Iowa. Although Wyatt was born and raised in the Midwest, he spent most of his life in the western part of the United States.

missed his brothers. So he tried to enlist. Wyatt didn't get far. He was quickly sent home for being too young. One account says that Wyatt's own father was the one who told him to go back to the farm.[2]

Nicholas left the army in 1864 and decided it was time for another change. He loaded up his family and joined a wagon train headed west to California. Wyatt drove one of the wagons and hunted for fresh meat for his family and the other travelers. Seven months later, the family reached San Bernardino, California. Nicholas bought a **ranch** and settled down.

Wyatt was not interested in settling down. Instead, he found a job as a **stagecoach** driver. In 1868, he traveled to Wyoming to help build the Union Pacific Railroad. Wyatt's skill with horses led him to a job handling the mule teams that graded, or flattened, the bed for the railroad tracks.

In 1870, Wyatt rejoined his family in Lamar, Missouri, where he became the town's **constable**. He married a young woman named Urilla Sutherland, but she died just a few months later. In March 1871, Wyatt was accused of collecting fees for the town but keeping the money for himself instead. Then a local man named James Cromwell said that Wyatt had cheated him out of the true value of some farm machinery Wyatt had taken as part of a court action. Wyatt never went to trial on either of these charges because no one could find him. He had left town.[3]

Wyatt joined a group that was mapping part of the country called Indian Territory. Later, this land would become the state of Oklahoma. Wyatt worked as a buffalo hunter, shooting them to provide meat for the rest of the group. He was a good shot and could handle any gun from a small pistol to a hunting rifle.

He got into more trouble while he was in Indian Territory. In April 1871, Wyatt and two other men were accused of stealing horses. Horses were extremely valuable in the West, so horse theft was a

As a young man, Wyatt hunted buffalo to provide food for men working in what is now Oklahoma. At this time, huge herds of buffalo roamed all over the plains, but within a few years, hunters like Buffalo Bill (shown here) wiped out most of the buffalo herds.

This painting shows a young man being tried for stealing horses. Horses were very valuable in the days before cars and trucks, and stealing horses was a serious crime.

very serious crime. Wyatt was arrested but escaped from jail and left town before a trial could be held.[4] The other two men were eventually **acquitted**.

At this point in his life, it seemed like Wyatt had a knack for ending up on the wrong side of the law. That was about to change.

A Kansas cowboy looks over his herd of cattle. Cowboys were responsible for driving huge herds of cattle from the plains to big cities in Kansas, where they were shipped to markets in the north and east.

CHAPTER 3

Trouble in Kansas

Wyatt Earp arrived in Kansas in 1873. At that time, Kansas was a wild, lawless place. Cowboys led **cattle drives** from Texas into the Kansas towns of Dodge City, Abilene, Ellsworth, and Wichita. These towns were major centers for the railroads, which shipped the cattle to markets in the north and east. Outlaws were always trying to steal these valuable cattle.

The cowboys themselves often caused trouble as well. They traveled with plenty of money, which they were happy to spend in the town's **saloons**. Alcohol was easy to find, and so were guns. It was not unusual for fights to break out, often with deadly results. Towns did not want to get rid of cowboys because they provided a lot of money to local businesses, but they did need strong lawmen to keep the peace. Western historian Lee A. Silva wrote, "This special breed of lawmen was made up of men who . . . had to be the toughest of the tough, for those who weren't were fated to end up in Boot Hill [dead], or if they lived long enough, be run out of town when their many flaws were soon ferreted out by the human renegades who lived merely to test the mettle of another man."[1]

When Wyatt Earp arrived in Ellsworth, Kansas, the town had such a bad reputation for violence that the *Kansas State News* once ran a headline stating "As we go to press, Hell is in session in Ellsworth."[2] In August 1873, Wyatt was gambling in a saloon in Ellsworth when the sheriff kicked two famous Texas gunfighters, Billy and Ben Thompson, out of the building. Billy's response was to shoot and kill the sheriff.

Ben Thompson told his brother to leave town while he gathered a large number of their friends to stop anyone from going after him. For more than an hour, Thompson stood in the street, holding a shotgun and a smaller gun known as a six-shooter while he dared anyone to go after his brother. Not even the town's lawmen were brave enough to go against Ben Thompson and his gang.

Ellsworth's mayor was furious that none of his deputies would challenge the gunfighter, so he fired all of them. When Wyatt volunteered to take down Ben Thompson, the mayor pinned one of the fired deputy's badges onto his shirt. Wyatt calmly took a pair of guns and walked into the street to face Thompson. As Thompson's men stood with their guns pointed toward him, Wyatt talked calmly to Thompson. The gunfighter realized that Wyatt was prepared to shoot him, so he surrendered. Later, Wyatt explained the moment by saying that being killed was "the chance any officer has to take and for the time being I was taking the place of an officer . . . I couldn't bear to see him get away with what he was doing. People have a right to live in peace."[3]

Wyatt was offered a job as a deputy in Ellsworth, but he declined and left town. By 1874, he was living in Wichita, Kansas, where he did accept a position as deputy marshal. Earp worked in Wichita for about two years. During that time he helped get rid of most of the lawlessness that had been present there.

In 1876, Wyatt moved on to become an assistant marshal in Dodge City, Kansas. As in Wichita, Wyatt did a good job of helping restore law and order to the wild town. Although later Wyatt would be seen as a man who never hesitated to shoot, the truth was that Wyatt had a better way to use his gun. Wyatt claimed that he had a specially made gun as a gift from Western writer Ned Buntline. The gun was called the Buntline Special, and it had an extra-long barrel. Wyatt called the gun his favorite, and always carried it with him.[4] The long barrel made it useful because Wyatt would use the gun to hit a troublemaker over the head. The bad guy would be knocked unconscious, and Wyatt could end any trouble without actually killing anyone. Once Wyatt had helped to tame Dodge City, it was time to move on again. He headed for Tombstone, Arizona.

An example of a Buntline Special, Earp's favorite kind of gun.

Statues of Wyatt Earp and his friend Doc Holliday stand in the Arizona train station where Wyatt's violent "Vendetta Ride" began.

CHAPTER **4**

From Lawman to Outlaw

Wyatt arrived in Tombstone in 1879. He joined his brothers, Virgil and Morgan, who were working in town as marshals. Wyatt was also joined by his old friend Doc Holliday. Doc once saved Wyatt's life in Dodge City when he shot a man who had crept up behind Wyatt and was about to shoot him in the back. Holliday was sick with a deadly disease called **tuberculosis**. He feared nothing and lived like he had nothing to lose.

Wyatt soon became a deputy US marshal. He wanted to become the sheriff of Tombstone, but instead, the governor appointed a man named John Behan. Wyatt and Behan did not get along. Wyatt especially distrusted Behan because he thought the sheriff was connected to a local gang led by the Clanton brothers. Another problem was that Behan and Wyatt were both in love with the same woman, Josie Marcus.

It didn't take long for trouble to start between Wyatt and the Clanton gang. In 1881, Wyatt accused the Clantons of robbing a stagecoach and stealing cattle. The bad feelings between the Earps and the Clantons reached a head on the night of

October 25. Ike Clanton and fellow gang member Tom McLaury got drunk and told everyone they wanted a showdown with the lawmen. Virgil and Wyatt tried to stop them, but it was too late. By late afternoon the following day, three men were dead and three were injured near the O.K. Corral. Several days later, Sheriff Behan arrested Wyatt, his brothers, and Doc Holliday for murder. Their trial became one of the biggest news stories in the country. A judge dismissed the case, saying that the Earps had not committed a crime.

The trouble didn't end with the trial. A few months later, Virgil Earp was **ambushed** and shot in the thigh and left arm. He almost died. The wounds were so serious that Virgil lost full use of his arm and walked with a limp for the rest of his life. Ike Clanton and his brother, Fin, were charged with attempted murder because Ike's hat was found near the shooting. However, the Clantons' friends told the judge that Ike was somewhere else at the time of the shooting, so he and Fin were found not guilty. Wyatt felt the law had failed him. So did the judge, William Stilwell. He told Wyatt, "You'll never clean up this crowd this way. Next time you'd better leave your prisoners out in the brush where **alibis** don't count."[1]

Then, in March 1882, several Clanton gang members fired through the window of a building where Wyatt and his brother Morgan were playing pool. Morgan was shot and died in Wyatt's arms.

Something changed in Wyatt after Morgan died. He didn't care about the law anymore. Wyatt wanted

revenge. His **vendetta** started the night he placed Morgan's body on a train to send it back to his parents' home in California. Virgil, who was still recovering from his injuries, was also on the train. As the train left the station, Wyatt spotted Ike Clanton and another man, Frank Stilwell, hiding along the tracks with rifles. Wyatt went after them and shot Stilwell to death. Ike Clanton got away, but Wyatt was not finished.

Over the next two weeks, Wyatt, his brother Warren, and Doc Holliday tracked down and killed two more men they believed had murdered Morgan. Newspapers all over the country followed Wyatt's every move. They called his efforts "the Vendetta Ride." Some people thought Wyatt was nothing more than a murderer who wanted revenge. Others believed he was simply fighting for justice.

When it was all over, Wyatt, Warren, and Doc were all outlaws. They left Tombstone and rode to Trinidad, Colorado. Wyatt's friend Bat Masterson was a marshal there. Masterson convinced Colorado's governor not to return the men to Tombstone. For Wyatt, his career as a lawman was over. Now he was an outlaw himself.

Wyatt and his wife, Josie, lived a fairly quiet life in California when they got older. This photo shows 75-year-old Wyatt in his home in 1923.

CHAPTER 5

Making a Myth

Wyatt spent the next few years on the move. For a while, he lived in Gunnison, Colorado, where he made money gambling. By the end of 1882, Wyatt and his brothers, Warren and Virgil, moved to San Francisco. There he met up with Josie Marcus, who had been his girlfriend back in Tombstone. Wyatt and Josie later married and were together for more than forty-five years, until Wyatt's death.

Wyatt and Josie bounced between Colorado, Idaho, and California for the next few years. Wyatt tried to find gold by buying several mines. He also ran a saloon. By 1896, the couple was back in San Francisco.

Wyatt, who was a fan of boxing, was asked to referee a match between Tom Sharkey and "Ruby Bob" Fitzsimmons. A crowd of 10,000 people gathered to watch the fight. It was one of the first matches fought under new rules, which included "no hitting below the belt." During the eighth round, Sharkey doubled over in pain. It looked like Fitzsimmons had hit him below the belt, so Wyatt ruled that Sharkey was the winner. However, many people believed Sharkey faked the injury. The crowd was angry at the outcome of the fight, and they took their hard feelings out on Wyatt. Newspapers wrote about his violent past and printed cartoons of Wyatt as an outlaw waving a gun.

Wyatt and Josie had had enough. They left San Francisco and moved to Alaska during the height of the gold rush there. Wyatt knew there was money to be made from the miners. He and Josie opened a saloon and were very successful.

By 1909, the Earps were living in Los Angeles. For years, Wyatt worked as an advisor on movies about the West and became friendly with several movie stars. He thought that a movie about his life would help convince people that he was a hero. He wrote to actor William S. Hart, who was famous for playing cowboys onscreen. Wyatt wrote, "If the story were exploited on the screen by you, it would do much toward setting me right before a public which has always been fed lies about me."[1] However, Hart never made a movie about Wyatt's life.

Wyatt was still famous, and it bothered him that many people thought he was a killer. He wanted to tell his side of the story, so in the late 1920s he contacted author Stuart Lake. Lake interviewed Wyatt and wrote a biography called *Wyatt Earp: Frontier Marshal*. The book was published soon after Wyatt's death and was a big success. The stories Lake told became the basis of the idea that Wyatt was a larger-than-life lawman.

Wyatt Earp died of the flu on January 13, 1929. He was eighty years old. In the years after his death, he got his wish of being seen as an American hero. Several movies and television programs were made about him and the Gunfight at the O.K. Corral, and he was the subject of many books. These books and movies portrayed Wyatt as a good guy who valued law and order above everything else. Although Wyatt did not live to see these images of himself, he probably would have been proud of them.

Wyatt and Josie's tombstone in Colma, California. The couple was married for more than forty-five years.

FACT OR FICTION?

Wyatt Earp said he did not regret what he did at the O.K. Corral or afterward. "For my handling of the situation at Tombstone, I have no regrets," he said. "Were it to be done again, I would do it exactly as I did it at the time."[1] Many people agree with Wyatt and view his actions as noble and heroic. It is true that he was a powerful figure of law and order. The crime rate dropped in every town where he worked as a lawman, and he usually managed to keep order without firing a shot.

Most people get their ideas about Wyatt through movies such as *My Darling Clementine* (1946), *Gunfight at the OK Corral* (1957), *Tombstone* (1993), and *Wyatt Earp* (1994), and the television series *The Life and Legend of Wyatt Earp* (1955–1961). They created an image of an American hero that was hard to deny. As writer Andrew Isenberg points out, "Justice, in this view, is found not in fickle courtrooms, but in the character of stalwarts such as Earp, who possess an innate sense of law and order. It is a view that suggests . . . that justice grows out of the barrel of a gun."[2]

Of course, movies and television shows are often one-sided and show only certain things about a person or an event. They also change the facts to make the story more interesting. For example, in the TV show *The Life and Legend of Wyatt Earp*, Wyatt gets into many shootouts with outlaws and is famous for how fast he can draw his gun. In real life, Wyatt preferred to knock out the bad guys rather than shoot them.

Many historians also question the accuracy of Stuart Lake's book. He exaggerated many details to make Wyatt look like more of a hero. The Thompson and Buntline stories may not have happened the way that Lake wrote. He even admitted that he made up many of the quotes Wyatt had supposedly said.

In real life, there are usually two sides to every story. While people think of Wyatt as a lawman, that's not all he was. In fact, Wyatt's career in law enforcement only lasted ten years. He spent most of his life running saloons, mining for gold and oil, and working at other jobs.

It also is not fair to show Wyatt as a good guy who never did anything wrong. He was charged with stealing horses as a young man. He liked to gamble and had friends who were not law-abiding citizens. And he did kill several men in his "Vendetta Ride." When Wyatt left Tombstone, he had a murder charge on his head. While it's true that Wyatt committed those murders to avenge his brothers, they are still murders.

Wyatt Earp was a fearless man who could keep outlaws from causing trouble through his presence alone. He was also a cold-hearted murderer who avenged his brothers' injuries and death through murder. So was Wyatt a hero or an outlaw? The fact is, he was both, and that is probably why he has fascinated Americans for more than one hundred years.

Chapter 1: Gunfight!

1. Josephine Earp, *I Married Wyatt Earp: The Recollections of Josephine Sarah Marcus Earp*, ed. Glenn G. Boyer (Tucson. AZ: University of Arizona Press, 1976), p. 28.

Chapter 2: Wyatt Wanders

1. "The American Experience: Wyatt Earp." PBS.org. http://www.pbs.org/wgbh/americanexperience/features/transcript/wyatt-transcript/
2. Darold Fredricks, "Wyatt Earp, the Man, the Myth, the Legend. *The Daily Journal*, February 15, 2010. http://archives.smdailyjournal.com/article_preview.php?id=125088
3. Steve Gatto, "Civil Complaints Against Wyatt Earp." The Wyatt Earp History Page. http://www.wyattearp.net/complaints.html
4. Steve Gatto, "Arkansas Horse Theft Charge." The Wyatt Earp History Page. http://www.wyattearp.net/arkansas.html

Chapter 3: Trouble in Kansas

1. Lee A. Silva, *Wyatt Earp: A Biography of the Legend, vol. 1, The Cowtown Years* (Santa Ana, CA: Graphic Publishers, 2002), p. 246.
2. Joseph Geringer, "Ellsworth." *Wyatt Earp: Knight with a Six-Shooter*. Court TV. http://www.crimelibrary.com/gangsters_outlaws/outlaws/earp/5.html

3. Casey Tefertiller, *Wyatt Earp: The Life Behind the Legend* (New York: John Wiley and Sons, 1997), p. 8.
4. Geringer, Joseph. "Doc Holliday." *Wyatt Earp: Knight with a Six-Shooter*. Court TV. http://www.crimelibrary.com/gangsters_outlaws/outlaws/earp/8.html

Chapter 4: From Lawman to Outlaw

1. "The American Experience: Wyatt Earp." PBS.org. http://www.pbs.org/wgbh/americanexperience/features/transcript/wyatt-transcript/

Chapter 5: Making a Myth

1. "The American Experience: Wyatt Earp." PBS.org. http://www.pbs.org/wgbh/americanexperience/features/transcript/wyatt-transcript/

Fact or Fiction

1. Joseph Geringer, "Doc Holliday." *Wyatt Earp: Knight with a Six-Shooter*. Court TV. http://www.crimelibrary.com/gangsters_outlaws/outlaws/earp/8.html
2. Isenberg, Andrew. "The Wyatt Earp Myth: America's Most Famous Vigilante Wasn't." *The Daily Beast*, July 21, 2013. http://www.thedailybeast.com/articles/2013/07/21/the-wyatt-earp-myth-america-s-most-famous-vigilante-wasn-t.html

acquitted (uh-KWI-tuhd)—found not guilty of a crime

alibis (AL-uh-biez)—proofs of being somewhere else at the time a crime was committed

ambush (AM-bush)—a surprise attack

avenge (uh-VENJ)—to get revenge on someone

cattle drives (KAT-uhl DRIVES)—when herds of cattle are moved from their grazing areas to the city where they will be taken to market

constable (KON-stuh-buhl)—a public officer in a town who is responsible for keeping the peace

corral (kuh-RAL)—a fenced area to keep horses or cattle

deputies (DEP-yoo-teez)—lawmen who assist a marshal or sheriff

marshal (MAR-shal)—a law enforcement officer

outlaws (OUT-lawz)—people who break the law

ranch (RANCH)—a place where people raise cattle

regret (ree-GRET)—to feel bad or sorry about something

revenge (ree-VENJ)—action a person takes to pay someone back for harm he or she has done to that person

saloons (suh-LOONZ)—bars; places where people go to drink

stagecoach (STAGE-koach)—a wagon pulled by horses and used to carry passengers or mail over long distances

tuberculosis (too-ber-kyoo-LOH-sis)—a serious disease that affects the lungs

vendetta (ven-DET-uh)—a series of violent actions taken for revenge

"The American Experience: Wyatt Earp." PBS.org. http://www.pbs.org/wgbh/americanexperience/features/transcript/wyatt-transcript/

Earp, Josephine. *I Married Wyatt Earp: The Recollections of Josephine Sarah Marcus Earp*, ed. Glenn G. Boyer. Tucson, AZ: University of Arizona Press, 1976.

Fredricks, Darold. "Wyatt Earp, the Man, the Myth, the Legend. *The Daily Journal*, February 15, 2010. http://archives.smdailyjournal.com/article_preview.php?id=125088

Gatto, Steve. The Wyatt Earp History Page. http://www.wyattearp.net/

Geringer, Joseph. *Wyatt Earp: Knight with a Six-Shooter*. Court TV. http://www.crimelibrary.com/gangsters_outlaws/outlaws/earp/1.html

Isenberg, Andrew. "The Wyatt Earp Myth: America's Most Famous Vigilante Wasn't." *The Daily Beast*, July 21, 2013. http://www.thedailybeast.com/articles/2013/07/21/the-wyatt-earp-myth-america-s-most-famous-vigilante-wasn-t.html

Ramsland, Katherine. "The U.S. Marshals: The Long Arm of the Law: The Tombstone Myth." Crime Library.com. http://www.crimelibrary.com/gangsters_outlaws/cops_others/us_marshals/3.html

Silva, Lee A. *Wyatt Earp: A Biography of the Legend, vol. 1, The Cowtown Years*. Santa Ana, CA: Graphic Publishers, 2002.

Tefertiller, Casey. *Wyatt Earp: The Life Behind the Legend*. New York: John Wiley and Sons, 1997.

"Wyatt Earp: Frontier Lawman of the American West." Legends of America.com http://www.legendsofamerica.com/we-wyattearp.html

FURTHER READING

_____. *History for Kids: The Illustrated Life of Wyatt Earp*. Kindle Edition. Cambridge, MA: Charles River Editors, 2013.

Epstein, Dwayne. *Lawmen of the Old West*. Farmington Hills, MI: Lucent Books, 2005.

Goodman, Michael E. *Wyatt Earp*. Mankato, MN: Creative Education, 2006.

Green, Carl R. and William R. Sanford. *Wyatt Earp*. Revised edition. Berkeley Heights, NJ: Enslow, 2009.

Urban, William. *Wyatt Earp: The O.K. Corral and the Law of the American West*. New York: Rosen, 2003.

Woog, Adam. *Wyatt Earp (Legends of the Wild West)*. New York: Chelsea, 2010.

ON THE INTERNET

Spartacus Educational: Wyatt Earp. http://spartacus-educational.com/WWearpW.htm

12 Things You Might Not Know About Wyatt Earp. http://www.neatorama.com/2012/11/08/12-Things-You-Might-Not-Know-About-Wyatt-Earp/#!bzvQS2

Wyatt Earp. http://www.history.com/topics/wyatt-earp

Wyatt Earp Biography. http://www.biography.com/people/wyatt-earp-9283338#synopsis

ABOUT THE AUTHOR

Joanne Mattern is the author of many books for children on a variety of subjects, including history and biography. She has written numerous biographies for Mitchell Lane. Joanne loves to learn about people, places, and events and bring historical figures to life for today's readers. She lives in New York State with her husband, children, and several pets.